The Heart of A Woman

An amazing way to speak to the hearts of Women and girls to help them release the hidden treasures of the heart.
A thirty day journey into the heart of a Woman.

Sundra-Wilson-Harris

The Heart Of A Woman
Copyright © 2020 By Sundra Wilson-Harris
All Rights Reserved

This book or any portion thereof may not be reproduced or used
in any manner whatsoever with the express written permission of the author
except for brief questions in a book review.
ISBN: 9780578666464

Content

1	Teach me how to pray A Prayer for Women and girls	7
2	The Story Behind The Story By Sundra L. Wilson- Harris	11
3	Morning Affirmations (Write down your Affirmations)	17
4	Self Love is important	27
5	A Love letter to Myself "The Heart Of A Woman"	31
6	A Love Letter To Yourself	35
7	The Hidden Treasures Of The Heart Is Revealed When You Speak (Matthew 12: 34-35)	41
8	Having A Heart To Reach Others	47
9	Where My Heartfelt Mission Began	53
10	Rejection Pushed Me Into My Purpose	63
11	Let Your Heart Speak (The Heart of A Woman Journal)	67
12	The Impact Of A Changed Heart	75
13	A Heart That Forgives	81
14	Who do you need to forgive?	89
15	My most heartbreaking moment	93
16	My Testimony	103
17	The Hidden Truth	111

Chapter 1

Teach me how to pray
A Prayer for Women and girls

A Prayer to start off your day:

Dear Lord,
Thank you for another day that wasn't promised. Thank you for life, health and strength. Thank you for every breath I breathe in and out. Thank you for the activities of my limbs. Thank you for keeping me in my right mind. Thank you for making me, molding me into the Woman I am today. I humble myself to be the vessel used in the earth realm to impact the lives of other Women and young girls. I make myself available for those who may need me today or any other day. Teach me how to pray. Teach me how to trust you more.

Increase my faith.

Thank you for every Woman reading this prayer. Thank you for her heart and for meeting her heart desires. Everything this Woman faces give her the courage to handle it. Give her the Wisdom and knowledge she needs to endure her toughest trials. Give her a heart of gold. Let her be a Woman of integrity. When others see her let them see the heart of God through her. Let her remember she is fearfully and wonderfully made. Let her impact the lives of other women she will see on her day to day journey.
In Jesus name.
Amen

Chapter 2

The story behind the story:

This story is inspired by my own story. As a little girl you dream of one day becoming successful. Not knowing it could be ruined within seconds. It's amazing that no matter how much chaos one could be around I didn't know that all the horrible things I experienced would be the very thing to mold me into the Woman I am today. Dealing with sexual abuse, mental abuse and physical abuse. Waking up from horrible nightmares and scared the world was ending because my own world felt like it had ended. I was afraid to the point as a little girl I would say "Lord please don't take me now I'm not ready". Not knowing in actuality I have to be ready when Jesus come. I didn't know until I was in my early twenties that the dreams I was having as a little girl was showing me step by step what I would be doing and how God would make a way of escape for me.

♡

I was damaged as a child and I thought when I become a Woman I would still be damaged. God had better plans for me. As a teenager I started looking for love in all the wrong places. I became a teen mother at the age of fifteen years old. No sense of direction and for a minute I thought I was the only one who had ever made that mistake. I had adults calling me out of my name. I had certain family members calling me out of my name. Saying to me "You'll never be nothing. Nobody will ever marry her". I'm so glad I didn't listen to those voices. Even though I had rebelled against God and had made such horrible choices in my life it never stopped Him from loving me.

I could still hear this soft voice saying "I have a plan".

As a teenager dealing with low self-esteem and depression I knew if I didn't start getting around someone who could uplift me I knew I wouldn't live to see my twenties. There was a Woman that came into my life. A Woman by the name of Joan Osborne. She is a Pastor in Dallas Texas. I call her my guardian angel. She never once misjudged me. She began to speak to the broken girl in me though I was a Woman dealing with brokenness. I had to heal from my past. My healing would one day impact the Woman I would soon become. I had my guard up very strong but that didn't stop Pastor Joan Osborne. This Woman would let me call her two, three o'clock in the morning when I was going through just to cry out to her. I know I got on her last nerve but it didn't matter to her.
She was determined to help me.

She taught me God cannot heal what I was not willing to reveal and how to be true to myself. As time went on she started teaching me to own my own wrongs as well. I wanted so bad to say and do mean things to others who had hurt me but she would remind me that in order to have the Character of God shown through me I must first humble myself and learn how to forgive others as well as myself. As I began to mature in my faith and my beliefs I took every golden nugget this Woman sowed into me and I started helping others.

I never thought I'd see that day come that I had so many broken Women come to me for advice. It's so important to have people in your corner to help you while you're broken. No one was ever meant to bear those burdens alone. We were meant to place them at the feet of Jesus Christ and He would bear those burdens for us. You must carry your cross and when you find yourself feeling as if you can't bear the weight of it because you feel as if you can't go on. God will send someone to help motivate you and push you. I'm thankful that God heard my cry even when I was silently crying within. There is motivation behind my story
" The Heart Of A Woman". I speak not from a broken place but from a heart that has been healed. I pray that everything I mention in this book will bring healing to every young lady and to Women around the world to never walk in shame of what you've been through. Let your voice be heard so that every generation of Women will see the glory of
God in your story just like me.

Chapter 3

Morning Affirmations

Day 1

1. I am bold and Confident.
2. I will not allow any negativity to corrupt my space.
3. I am loved and I will spread love.
4. I am enough.
5. I feel healthy and I am strong.
6. Today I will think good thoughts.
7. Let it go.
8. Forgive others quickly and forgive yourself.
9. Believe in yourself.
10. I have a purpose.
11. I am blessed and highly favored.
12. Trust the process.
13. Make each day count.
14. I have enough knowledge to make better decisions for myself.
15. I am courageous and I am willing to face my fears.

Morning Affirmations

Day 2

1. Today is going to be a great day.
2. I am smart, kind and loved.
3. I am valuable
4. I have learned to trust the journey and path God has before me.
5. I will surround myself with people who will push me to be the best me.
6. I am more than a conqueror.
7. I believe in the person staring back at me in the mirror.
8. I am fearfully and wonderfully made.
9. I am beautiful, strong , and powerful.
10. I inspire those around me.
11. Every person attached to me is a winner.
12. I inhale confidence and exhale insecurities.

Morning Affirmations

Day 3

1. I welcome today with open arms.
2. I am whole and complete.
3. Today good things will happen for me.
4. I choose to fill myself with positivity.
5. I am an unstoppable force who can achieve anything.
6. I am my greatest competitor.
7. Today nothing shall by any means stop me.
8. Be Kind to others.
9. I am in control of my thoughts and feelings.
10. I make a difference in this world.

Morning Affirmations

Day 4

Today I want you to write down your own affirmations. I truly believe what we speak about ourselves we start to believe about ourselves. Get up and wash your face. Look at yourself in the mirror. Give yourself a smile. Now speak life into your life by speaking positive affirmations.

1. _____
2. _____
3. _____
4. _____
5. _____
6. _____
7. _____
8. _____
9. _____
10. _____

How do you feel after writing your affirmations down? You should be able to handle today with flying colors. You spoke over your own life and you believe what you say about your own self. It's so important to always believe in you and what you speak about you. When you truly know who you are. No one can ever convince you from believing in you.

Chapter 4
Self Love Is Important

Often times we as Women have dealt a bad hand in life. We never take the time to love ourselves. We find ourselves being good for others and we're never good to ourselves.
I had to learn that even in a broken place in my life I was no good for others who needed me until I was good to myself . Putting yourself first is not being selfish. I learned to embrace self love. Was it easy? Not at all. I had to let go of past trauma and wounds. Dealing with that was very hard for me. It made it hard for me to trust others as well. In hard times like that you need other strong people around you to help you through that. When I learned to let go of things that affected me in my past I had the strength to move past it all.

Think about it. What are some things that you know affected you in your past that you thought you let go of that haunts you to this day? What are your triggers that make you think back to those negative past incidents?
Write them down below.

1._____

2._____

3._____

4._____

5._____

6._____

7._____

8._____

9._____

10._____

After you thought about it, was it really worth holding on to? Not at all. Forgiveness plays a huge part in your healing. Sometimes people don't realize that
forgiveness is for yourself as well as those who have hurt you. There's a scripture I'm reminded of that says:

"For you O Lord, are good and forgiving, abounding in steadfast love to all who call upon you."

Psalm 86:5

I feel that just as we expect the Lord to forgive us we too should forgive others. He loves us with an everlasting love and He forgives us with his mercy that endures forever.

Chapter 5

A Love Letter To My Self

Hey beautiful,
I see you're still fighting the good fight of faith. You're conquering the world each morning you awake. I saw the tears fill your eyes the moment you took your first look in the mirror to see yourself. You don't look like what you've been through. It is by the grace of God you wipe those tears and look fear in the eyes as it secretly appeared. Without doubt you knew God had your back because you woke up determined not to ever lookback.

♡

Hey beautiful I am mesmerized by your courage that you seem to embrace. Creating new chapters of your life story and God's amazing grace. Never lose your voice to a generation who need to hear that there is hope. The Woman that's afraid to speak her heart needs to know that she's free to speak no matter what she goes through. She must be reminded that this too shall pass. Someone is counting on you today so set aside all your worries and doubts. Remind fear that you're the David that will knock any giant out. One smooth stone of self love, self confidence and self worth. That's all it will take to knock that giant of fear on it's back because this Woman knows her worth.

The Heart Of A Woman

I am smart, I am beautiful and I feel really confident about who I am. By any means necessary nothing and I do mean nothing will ever take this Godfidence I wear it well. It is my crown. I am a God fearing Woman who has potential and class. I promise I'm living each day like it's my last. I'm living my life like it's golden. I'm free and no longer bound by those obstacles that were sent to destroy me.

I love you and who you are becoming. Keep soaring higher and higher. Never looking back but moving forward in the promises of God.

"The Heart Of A Woman"

The Heart Of A Woman

Chapter 6

A Love Letter To Yourself

Now you've read my love letter to myself.

Take this time to write a beautiful letter to encourage yourself.

_____

_____

_____

_____

_____

_____

_____

The Heart Of A Woman

The Heart Of A Woman

The Heart Of A Woman

The Heart Of A Woman

Chapter 7
The Hidden Treasures Of The Heart Is Revealed When You Speak

I never knew that what you speak out of your mouth comes from your heart. I read it in the scriptures:

Matthew 12:34 says For out of the abundance of the heart the mouth speaks. I would hear people say some of the rudest things and after they say it they would cover it up with "I'm just playing ". It made me reevaluate myself. I was so careful on how I say things and I made sure that whatever
I said I was truly ready to say it.
We don't realize how powerful our words are.

Proverbs 18:21

Death and life are in the power of the tongue: and they that love it shall eat the fruit thereof.

I have learned so much while getting understanding of the scriptures. To know what I speak it will manifest. Now that I have complete understanding I have to make sure anything I speak it must be good and I must speak life. What if the things that are manifesting in our life is coming from things we have spoken over ourselves?

The scriptures tell us in James 1:19

Wherefore, my beloved brethren, let every man be swift to hear, slow to speak, slow to wrath. It's so clear to me that we should always be willing to hear before speaking and getting caught up in anger so quickly about anything.
It completely shows us how powerful our words are, how powerful our thoughts can be and how it's important to respond the right way.

If you could change something you've reacted to in a negative way how would you handle it differently?

_____
_____
_____
_____
_____
_____
_____
_____
_____
_____
_____
_____
_____
_____

The Heart Of A Woman

Chapter 8

Having A Heart to Reach Others

In order to help others, it must first be in your heart to do so. I remember at the age of 16 years old I got my first job working as a cashier at a restaurant. I remember the day I received my first check I was able to not only help my mom but I remember seeing this homeless man holding up a sign saying "Will work for food". I saw this man who was not asking for cash but was asking for help to get him something to eat. I remember telling my mom to take me up to Churches Chicken so I could get this man something to eat.
It wasn't for show it was because it was already in my heart to help someone in need.

As a young girl I watched my grandparents helping people and feeding people and making a difference in our community. To see people smiling over receiving food or just kind words of encouragement made my heart very glad. I knew one day God would open up a door for me to do the same thing. I am left to carry their legacy and impact communities as well and to help those in need. It has to come from the heart in order for you to flow freely in giving. I always share with my children how much more blesseth it is to give than to receive.

I love to help others because I know what we do here brings glory and honor to God. What I have read in the scriptures it is clearly stated that we are here to help others who are in need.

Matthew 25:35-36 KJV

For I was hungry, and ye gave me meat: I was thirsty, and ye gave me drink: I was a stranger, and ye took me in: Naked, and ye clothed me: I was sick, and ye visited me: I was in prison, and ye came unto me.

When I read this I then understood the mission my grandparents were trying to accomplish before leaving here. I see it is a mission we must all achieve. I stay humble in what God has afforded me to do because I saw in the scriptures and did understand that whatever I do to help others will reflect the character of who our God truly is. So make sure you have a heart to reach others by way of helping others.

It truly is a blessing to help others.

What ever is in your heart is identified by your actions.

Chapter 9

Where My Heart Felt Mission Began

I remember the day the Lord gave me an assignment that would not only affect the lives of Women of all nationalities but of young girls as well. Believe it or not my ministry started in my home in my living room. I was called to help Women. Women who had been broken, struggling with self love and those who were trying to get a break through in such difficult times. I remember calling my friend Elesley Hardison. I began to share with her the vision God had given me. To me it didn't make any sense to start a ministry in my living room.

I had to trust what God was showing me and without any more doubt trust what He was guiding my feet to do. I remember reaching out and my friend with no hesitation believed it as well because she too had a desire to help bring Women together. We started inviting Women not only from our church but other Women we knew who would enjoy the fellowship and life changing gatherings. It went from being just a few Women to being a lot of women, children and men. Yes can you believe that? We had men come in and they too were blessed by it as well as the children. It began to get so huge I had no room left in my living room or dining area. Now that's the living proof when God tells you to do something that doesn't make any sense and he multiplies it by drawing more people to it than we had ever expected it to be.

Then in 2015 I started a group on Facebook called " Help A Sista Out". This group was developed to inspire Women all over the world that I have known or have never met. I want to reach the masses of Women no matter their background, race or age. I thought about every Woman in this world who would wake up feeling down and out that if they could open this group up and be motivated it would help change the way they were thinking at that moment and start their day off with motivation.
I have blessed Women in this group by a way of being pampered. Just to have some me time. I thought about how relaxing it is to get a manicure and a pedicure.

So in order for me to be fair I would have a drawing of the Women who we would shoutout on our Wednesday Courageous Women's day.
I started Wednesday Courageous Women's day because I wanted Women to see it's good to uplift other Women and to compliment one another . I wanted them to see that motivation is the key to uplifting someone's spirit who may be feeling down. I understand that we have no idea of what people are going through in this world. Don't let others who may be in a storm draw you into their storm but draw them into your peace. It has truly been a blessing waking up to motivate over two thousand Women a day.

The Heart Of A Woman

In 2017
I started a Nonprofit Organization called
"Dream Girlz Mentorship".
I wanted to help other young girls to never make the mistakes I made in life. To help redirect them into successful areas I had dreamed of achieving. I watch a lot of teen mothers who often are not the one's raising their babies look so down and left out when they see their friends who have no children be able to enjoy themselves. I could relate to the feelings as well. I look at the expressions on their faces and I see them feeling as if they're no longer a fit into their circle because they didn't think before making the choices they made. I don't want any more young girls making decisions before thinking of what the consequences will be based on the
decisions they will make in life.

I believe if I had a mentor at an early age or guidance I would have never made the choices I made. I was looking for a void to be filled. I was looking for love. I had been violated, overlooked and no one heard me crying out. So the moment I thought I was getting attention from someone it came with consequences. I knew that it was no longer about me but about my child that did not ask to be here. I want more young ladies to know their worth. I didn't see the value of my worth until God opened my eyes to identify who I really was as a person. If I could go back and speak to my younger self I would tell her your worth is far more than rubies.

I would tell her that everything she had to endure was the start of her story. God was rewriting my story. Though it started off as a nightmare I know it will bring a victorious ending to my story. Everything I had to endure in each chapter of my life helped made me the Woman I am today.

Take the time below and write a heartfelt letter to your younger self. What would you say to the young boy or girl who had to deal with having such a huge void in his/her life that left you speechless? Now is the time to let your voice be heard and release what you were never able to express. When you carry hurt from your past into your future you attach that hurt to those who are connected to you.
You will hurt those who want to love you because you have not healed from the hurt of your past.

_____

_____

_____

_____

_____

_____

_____

_____

The Heart Of A Woman

Chapter 10

Rejection Pushed Me into My Purpose

Many of you know my story. I never knew that rejection was God's protection. I have been rejected so much throughout my life I had to be delivered from a spirit of rejection. The rejection I received from my mother, my father and my brothers had me so guarded I didn't realize it had me afraid to be rejected by others. That was one of the toughest things I had to deal with in life. Talk about a hard pill to swallow that was hard. I was so afraid to the point I thought everyone that came into my life was going to reject me. It had me in a place of doubting who I could be. I'm so glad God took all those doubts and worries away. He had to let me see that the rejection I was encountering was to help develop me to accept it when I go out in the world to help others. Some would accept the help and some will reject it.

The rejection I had to endure from my mother, father and brothers God had to protect me and prepare me for what was about to come.
I would try to show my mother love. She was wounded. I didn't understand her rejection towards me. I found out that she too had been violated at a young age. How could she help me when she felt helpless herself? God had to open my ears to hear her and my eyes to see her so I could understand the rejection from her. God was protecting me in the midst of the rejection so I would be able to help her in areas she was not able to heal from. The hurt I carried I didn't realize I was carrying my cross to become the sacrifice to help bring healing not only for myself or my mother but to other Women who would have to bear their cross due to rejection, being misunderstood and left wounded.

My father just opened up to me about his wounded childhood and he too dealt a hard life which caused him to reject true love. God had to take me back as deep as my parents' past to pluck up and uproot the rejection that creeped into their past lives. God had to break that cycle that tried to attach itself into my life. Every generational curse stops with me. I will not allow it to go into another generation in my bloodline. I'm so thankful to God that my children don't have to deal with those horrible issues I had to deal with. I thank God everyday and I'm so thankful I don't look like what I've been through.

Chapter 11

Let Your Heart Speak
(The Heart Of A Woman Journal)

There's nothing like a good journal to have to write in everyday. For me writing is very therapeutic.
You never know how much tension you have or how stressful you've allowed yourself to become until you release it.
Prayer and writing always seems to help me. I want you to take a moment and focus. I want you to think deeply about some things that you truly have hidden in your heart that you have not released out of you. Let the issues of your heart flow.

If you want to write down some goals that you would like to achieve. Whatever you do, never lose sight of who you are and who you are becoming.
Now "Let Your Heart Speak". This is a personal moment to release the heart of the matter.

_____

_____

_____

_____

_____

_____

_____

_____

_____

_____

_____

The Heart Of A Woman

The Heart Of A Woman

The Heart Of A Woman

The Heart Of A Woman

Prayer

Heavenly Father,

I want to first say "Thank You". You have been better to me than I've been to myself. Thank you for mending broken hearts through the people who will encounter this book. Let it be life changing. Let it release those who have so many things bottled up within that as they release what's internalized healing would begin to take place in their lives. Lord bless people to open up and be free from things that have them bound. Let us not be weary in well doing. Heal more broken hearts so that more people will love like never before. Teach us how to let go and trust you even when we're struggling with trusting anyone. Let the wounds of our past be healed so we can embrace our freedom you've so freely given us. Let not our minds take us to a low place of thinking. Let us think good thoughts everyday. Help us to speak life. Let us awake each day and command our day to be great.Let us have more will power, but let our will line up with your will.
We put away childish things and embrace our maturity and new self. Thank you for letting us do more than exist. Thank you for opening the right doors for us and closing all the wrong doors behind us.
Let not our hearts be troubled. Let our hearts be filled with joy that only you can give us. Let us always be kind and gentle to one another.
Let our stories bring glory and honor to you.
In Jesus name. Amen.

Chapter 12

The Impact Of A Changed Heart

If you could reflect back and change something about yourself what would it be?

_____

_____

_____

_____

_____

_____

Oftentimes as women we can be so hard on ourselves. We forgive others and the mistakes they've made and we tend to forget to forgive ourselves. Sometimes we don't realize we are our worst critics. Why do we not see the good in ourselves like we do others? I have noticed over the years our biggest downfall is comparison. I want to be myself. I don't ever want to be like anyone else. I believe God uniquely made just one of us on purpose. You were never meant to be anyone but you.
I love to compliment other women.
I see so many beautiful women walking around with their heads down or just being bitter for no reason. I remember my days of being like that. It took another person with a heart of gold to speak into my life. I want to pay it forward and do the same.

It's not easy approaching women when they're like that. I'm so glad that I've learned to be nice to others, give them a smile and ask them how are you? Sometimes we don't realize simple hellos and have a nice day is the key to open doors of communication. Once people are comfortable with you they'll express their deepest feelings to you. It's never easy opening up to just anyone. I've had my heart broken many times sharing things with people who I thought I could trust. Only to be let down once they got upset with me by releasing my heart felt secrets. When it comes to it I take this matter seriously.

The Heart Of A Woman

I never want others to feel the heart aches I've had to endure. Once your trust with an individual is broken it's very hard to trust again. I'm so glad God healed me from that. No heart should be shattered. Not one time when I cried out to God did he leave my heart into pieces. I want to help as many broken hearts as possible. I want people to see my life as a testimony. I thank God for giving me not only a new heart but a change of heart. I will always see the good in others that never took the time to see good in me. I pray the change others see in me will impact the hearts of others to change.

Chapter 13

A Heart That Forgives

I shared with others about some hardships I had to endure in my past. I also shared some heart breaks as well. Never did I think in a million years that I could or would be able to forgive the people that hurt me deeply. I was left empty and wounded and treated like the black sheep in my family for confessing I was molested by a family member. I remember feeling cold and empty. I still had to look that individual in the face while he pretended that he didn't do anything to me. One day something tragic happened to him and I remember I cried so hard. I didn't want him to die though he killed every bit of confidence in me and made me feel like I was nothing. I prayed and asked God "Don't let him die".

♡

A part of me was thinking well maybe he should but then I thought to myself I wouldn't want anyone to wish that upon me. So I humbled myself and again I cried out to God
"Don't let him die".
Deep down inside I knew I had to forgive him.
If he had died in the accident how could I let him know I forgive him. I remember going up to his bedside praying over him and I said to him "I Forgive You".
It was at that moment I felt my heart beating again.
I felt a release I had never felt before.
I could literally feel the love of God covering me.

I never knew I had a heart to forgive until then. I was misjudged for being so guarded and no one ever took the time to ask my why was I being that way. People misjudged me and thought I was being mean. This is exactly why I don't misjudge people who are having a bad day. We have no clue about what others are going through. I couldn't believe I forgave the man that violated me in my childhood. I had someone question me and said why didn't you tell anyone?
Why did you wait until now?
They had no clue. I did tell someone. I told my mother but she was so broken and couldn't help me
because she was hiding the same secret inside herself.
She too had gone through it.
My mom had gone through so much she had become bitter.
Her response to me was
"So what, it happened to me; get over it".

I didn't understand her reply because in my mind I was thinking my mom was my protector because I didn't have my father there. Later on as time went on and when God healed me from that horrible hurt I was able to understand my mother's response. My mother had been violated the same way and no one was there to help her through it. Now that I've been helping other women who are opening up about their sexual abuse I have made it my business to make sure I help free my mother from her wounds she have carried for so many years. It's amazing how God had to open up my eyes to see my mom through a different lens. That's how I was able to open up to my mom with understanding the load of carrying that kind of hurt alone. I was so hurt and angry at first with my parents because I thought why didn't you both protect me?

The moment God saved me from myself I had to forgive them as well. All that I was faced with in my childhood made me very careful with my children. I was so strict with letting them spend the night over to their friends house or certain family members all because I didn't want what happened to me to happen to my children. It was my job to protect them even when no one protected me. As my children got older I explained to them why I was so guarded when it came down to anything pertaining to them. I say all the time God thank you for never letting my children go through that type of pain. I know many Women who are secretly dealing with this.
Thank God for a heart that forgives.

Now that I've been healed from my past I can help more Women move forward and lead them to the one and only God who can heal the brokenness inside they've had to carry. For the first time ever my mom told me while we were in a really deep conversation that she really needed help and she would like me to help her get through it. My heart melted because I never thought my boldness to stand up for myself would only save
other Women who lost their voice to cry out but to help this beautiful Woman who had carried me nine months. My mom has no clue how much I love her and adore her. I'm so glad that I can be her example to remind her of just how strong she really is. The enemy didn't win. I found my purpose in my pain.
I thank God each day for giving me a forgiving heart.
God blessed me with four sons and one daughter. Believe me when I say I owe God my life because he not only brought me out of a dark place. He saved and protected my children from what was sent to destroy me.
I'm truly blessed to still be here to tell my story.
"The Heart Of A Woman".

Chapter 14

Who Do You Need To Forgive?

I want you to take this time to forgive the people or that one individual who hurt you so deeply. This part will be hard at first but if you have to start here start the process of forgiving them now. You will be so happy that you did. Don't miss your blessing by trying to teach them a lesson.
Forgive them and be free.
Let me help you start it off.

Dear _____, (Place their name here.)

_____

_____

_____

_____

_____

_____

_____

_____

_____

_____

_____

_____

_____

_____

The Heart Of A Woman

Chapter 15

My Most Heartbreaking Moment

I've had my heart broken many times in my life. Losing my grandparents who I adored my entire life. I lost my grandmother Bertha Mae Wilson. I didn't think I could go on because I had never lost someone this close to me. This woman would give me the world if she could and now I'm sitting at her bedside losing her to cancer. Then not long after that I lost my grandfather William Wilson. Then losing my Big Mama Almetta Sanders really hit me hard. She was the woman who I saw kneeling at her bed every night praying. Watching her taught me how important it is to pray without ceasing. I always wondered why she had so many bibles by her bed.

♡

She was truly a woman of God. She was a great wife who stood by her husband and was the best mother, grandmother and great grandmother you could ever imagine. She was the example of a wife I knew one day I would be. She was my living example so when I lost her I thought to myself what am I going to do now? I lost one of my first cousins to violence and two months after that the most heartbreaking moment happened that I never expected. I lost my little sister. My mom named her "Tonya Rochelle Wilson". I lost my sister in the worst way I could ever imagine. We had spent the whole day together on Christmas in 2005. It was something about that day that just didn't seem right but we were so happy just being together.

I wasn't feeling too good that day so I asked my sister to bring me something back that I needed. I noticed the whole day she kept watching me. She came back but when she returned she had a camera with her. She told me let's make some memories with our children. So she went outside taking pictures of our children riding their bikes and playing. I noticed she kept coming into the room where I was just to take my picture. What really got me is she stood in the door just stirring at me as if it was her first or last time seeing me. I didn't put too much thought into it because I thought she's just making memories but not realizing she was making memories of us all being together for the last time. My mom cooked so much food that day. It was really good. We blessed the food, ate and I was ready to go rest.

I wasn't feeling well. My husband, the children and I were leaving to go home. I was so ready to lay down. Just as I was laying down I closed my eyes and my phone rings.
It was my sister Tonya. I said hello. If you really know my sister you would know she was talking really loud in my ear.
She said Sundra what are you doing? I replied
" I'm in bed". It's getting late, what are you doing up?
She began to tell me that our nephew we hadn't seen in a while was down here visiting and that I needed to come meet her to see him. I tried my best to talk myself out of going but Tonya wasn't taking no for an answer. I got up and put on my clothes so that I could go back to my mom's house to meet my sister there to meet my nephew. When I arrived I noticed I didn't see my sister's car there. I went in and surely I had beat my sister back to my moms house. I picked up the phone and called her.

She says "I'm on my way". Now I still didn't understand how I beat her there and she was just around the corner.
I began to pick up my nephew and play with him and finally my sister showed up talking loud as usual.
I never knew that the moment she sat down next to me it would be my last time seeing her. We laughed and talked for the longest and I looked at the time and noticed it was almost 1a.m.
I told her I had to go because it's getting late. I remember telling her my husband wanted me to bring him some cake back but he didn't need it. My sister loved her brother in law so she insisted that I needed to get him whatever he wanted and made sure I took my husband some cake back with me.

What really stuck with me that night my sister as she sat by me my nephew came up to me and my sister Tonya and put our hands together. He repeatedly did it three times. I remember as we were holding hands we looked at each other and laughed. I never thought in a million years that would be the last time I held her hand and saw her smile. I finally left my mom's house and went home only to be awakened by a phone call around 4 a.m. from my mom screaming "She's gone". It was like my whole world had stopped. My heart was beating so fast I couldn't think. I could hear my mom saying " He shot her". She was saying it over and over. I told my husband I have to go, mom said he killed my sister. I didn't know the whole details of what was going on but I was driving so fast I almost ran my car through the railroad railings trying to get to my sisters home. I saw so many police and ambulance lights going towards my mom's house.

It was then that I realized it must be true. Talk about a nightmare. I screamed and tried to run in her house but the police officers grabbed me and said I couldn't go in. They said you don't want to see her that way. They were right. I had to calm myself down at that moment and I remember looking up in the sky screaming "God I trust you ". I felt the peace of God come over me. I had no choice but to trust God because if I know anything I know God doesn't make any mistakes. This was the most heartbreaking moment for me because weeks before this my sister wrote me a four page letter. She was telling me how much she looked up to me and how when she grew up she wanted to be just like me. She told me she was proud of me because I had changed my life and I was serving God. She told me you are a wonderful mother to my niece and nephews and a great wife to your husband.

She said I know you only get on to me because you want what is best for me. She said even when you think I'm not listening to you I really am. I had to think about all she had told me in that four page letter and humble myself. I remember the police officer looking at me in amazement because I was calming down. He started encouraging me as well. I had no idea my two beautiful nieces were right there when this young man took their mother's life and he also took his own life right in front of them. Every day I would wake up hoping it was a horrible dream I was waking up from but it was real. This was one of my most heartbreaking moments but it was also in this moment God took me in my brokenness and began to rebuild me again. His strength is made perfect in our weakness.
I never took life for granted from that day on. I thought at first how would we ever see Christmas the same again?

Ever since we lost my sister the day after Christmas in 2005 I make sure each year we celebrate with my children and my sister's four beautiful children. God has truly blessed us to heal over the years. As long as I am here I will never let my sister Tonya be forgotten. She would be so proud of her children. I'm so proud of my nieces Dashundra & Lashonia Wilson. Them seeing their mother's life taken right in front of them could've mentally destroyed them but God protected them and brought healing to them in that difficult moment. They've both graduated high school and they're both in college. They're proof God can keep you and mend your broken heart. I thank God everyday for pulling me and my family through that heartbreaking day that we'll never forget.

Chapter 16

My Testimony

Even though I had a tough childhood and some tough times in life I don't look like what I've been through. I've been Married now to my Husband James Harris for twenty years.
I have four amazing sons
Johnt'a Wilson, Dartannon Wilson, D'erren Wilson,
Nakia Wilson-Harris and one amazing beautiful daughter
Nakaya Wilson-Harris. I have a beautiful grandson.
We call him Deray. It's so amazing because my grandson
Dartannon Deray Wilson Jr. was born the day my last two
(the twins) graduated high school.
That's the day I realized that a new chapter had begun.
I became this beautiful little boy's GiGi.

I am also proud of my two sons. Dartannon is a graduate from Texas A&M of Commerce and D'erren is a graduate of Wagner College in New York. They both graduated college with their bachelors degrees. It's because of them I was able to experience what college was all about. I honestly felt like I was a teenager again. They're the first in my family to go to college and graduate college. I'm one proud mother. I turned over a new leaf in my life. The day I said yes to God my life has not been the same. I almost gave up but I'm so glad I didn't throw in the towel. I didn't even let my critics convince me that I wasn't good enough. I'm very proud of myself. I raised my children and brought them up in the way they should go.

I made sure I kept them in church. Even though I hit some rough patches in my marriage I'm so glad my husband and I with God on our side made it through that as well. I started a Nonprofit Organization. I wrote my first book and am already writing my second one. I'm fighting the good fight of faith and overcoming heart disease. I'm still here. I'm alive and I survived every storm that was sent to destroy me. I made it by the grace of God and so will you. Thanks to everyone who believes in me. Thank you to all those who pray for me and my family. Thank you for letting this Woman speak her truth straight from the heart.
This is "The Heart Of A Woman ".

Affirmations

1. Think good thoughts.

2. Believe in yourself.

3. I have all faith and no fear.

4. Keep God first in everything.

5. Command your day to be great!

Words Of Encouragement

"You really haven't completed the circle of success until you've helped somebody else....."

Chapter 17

The Hidden Truth

Sometimes we think we are able to go on and pretend like we have it all together. Deep within there's someone suffering in silence. Have you ever tried to express your truth to someone and they didn't believe you? Have you ever been misjudged by people who had already labeled you based on what they've heard about you? Being judgmental gets us nowhere. We have to ask God to give us a heart to see others despite their past.

We need His eyes and heart of compassion. There is some hidden truth in you but in order to be free you must find what you've never freed yourself from. Find your truth below from the list I have written out for you.

What heartfelt hurts have you not released within? Underline or circle your hidden truth you have not released.

Circle Your Hidden Truth

1. I deal with low self esteem.

2. I have had thoughts of suicide.

3. I don't like who I have become.

4. I don't feel beautiful.

5. I have been sexually abused by a family member or someone I once trusted.

6. I feel stuck and unsupported.

7. I was told I would never be nothing.

8. I don't have a relationship with my parents.

9. I don't feel like I'm good enough.

10. I lost someone close to me and I never said goodbye.

11. I suffer in silence.

12. I don't know how to forgive.

13. I don't understand my purpose.

14. I don't know how to forgive myself.

15. I want revenge against people who have hurt me.

How many did you see yourself in? Now how did you feel after you admitted your truth? That's why it is so important to release those hurtful moments and deal with the heart of the matter. Never let that hurt turn you into a monster. Let it motivate you so that you can be a blessing to others. Be the best you and always be true to thine own self first.

My Bio Of My Story

Dealing with heart felt issues can sometimes be the hardest.
If it was left up to most people who deal with heartbreaking issues they would rather keep that hurt buried within.
Today is your day to be free.
Are you afraid to open up about your past hurts of sexual abuse, mental or physical abuse? Have your heart ever been shattered by the loss of a loved one? Have you ever been hurt by someone to a point you never thought you could
ever forgive them?
This book was written not only to tell my truth of brokenness.
It's to demonstrate God's healing and strength in my life.
It was written to help others see that there is healing after you've been shattered to pieces.
You will find inspiration and ways to help free you from being silent. You too have a voice to be heard and you should no longer suffer in silence. You will find healing through speaking life over yourself . You will find strength through words of daily affirmations. More importantly you will have the heart to forgive yourself and those who have wronged you.
God can't heal what you are not willing to reveal.
I pray that you will be inspired to reveal every broken place within so you can live in your truth and fulfill
your God given purpose.

The Heart Of A Woman

Dedication

This book is dedicated to my husband James Harris, my five children Johnt'a Wilson, Dartannon Wilson. D'Erren Wilson, Nakaya Wilson-Harris, Nakia Wilson-Harris, and to my first grandson Dartannon Deray Wilson Jr. also my bonus grandson D'Angelo Vasquez. I have always wanted to leave you all with something close to my heart. My very own story. To leave you with the golden nuggets of my truth that only I can tell from the bottom of my heart. You all hold a special part in my heart. You are all connected to me in such a special way. To my one and only daughter Nakaya. I want you to be as strong as I have become. Know that you are fearfully and wonderfully made. You are everything I prayed and asked God to let you be. You're beautiful, strong, intelligent and you have a heart of gold. Your beauty radiates in your smile. Never be afraid to have a voice in this world so that other young ladies will have one. Your beauty is skin deep. Look in the mirror and look past that beautiful face and skin. It's the beautiful treasures you have hidden within your heart. I want you to not only carry my legacy but build a legacy of your own. To all five of my children. Remember you are not only here to exist but you are here to leave your mark in this world and help be the change it needs to be. To my son Dartannon. Thank you for pushing me when I had no strength in me to go on. I never believed in myself enough to think I could accomplish anything until I had you all. The fruit of my labor is proven through my five amazing beautiful children. To my nieces Dashundra, Lashonia, and Ashanti. I'm so proud of y'all. You are all I have left of my sister Tonya (R.I.P.). I want you all to know every chance I have to be with y'all is like spending it with her. Continue to achieve and do great things. To my husband James. I thank you for sticking by me. You knew I was wounded and not one time did you misjudge me or leave me. I call you my Superman because it takes a super awesome guy like you to help bring me into a safe place. I thought I would never trust or love again. With you I was able to do just that. Thank you for being the man I've always prayed you would be. I believe in you as well as you believe in me. Thank you again.

The Heart Of A Woman

www.ingramcontent.com/pod-product-compliance
Lightning Source LLC
Chambersburg PA
CBHW071408290426
44108CB00014B/1726